Meg's Scrapbook

by Zoë Clarke

illustrated by Tania Rex

OXFORD
UNIVERSITY PRESS

Meg liked to help Gran on her farm.
They fixed lots of things.

Gran planted trees in the garden.
Meg picked lots of plums.

Meg chatted to Gran as she drank her milk.

Gran handed Meg a scrapbook.

“Stick things in so you do not forget,” said Gran.

Meg liked that plan. She started her Do-Not-Forget scrapbook.

She turned part of the scrapbook into a map.

Meg added things she spotted at the farm.

Meg painted Gran. Then she painted Fred and Alex. They helped in the farm shop.

Meg spilled some food on the scrapbook.

"You can put food things in that part," Gran said.

Meg jotted down cooking tips from Gran.

"I will stick them in," Meg said.

Meg crammed twigs and seeds into the book.

Soon the book did not shut! Gran helped Meg with some string.

"You can start a harvest scrapbook next," Gran said.

Meg nodded to agree.

"I will do that when I come back," Meg said. "I will not forget!"

Encourage students to review the things Meg included in her scrapbook.